Super Sharks

Emma Lynch

Ginn

Come on, dive in!

Would you want to come face to face with a shark? Probably not. But sharks are fascinating! They are the bad boys of the ocean and can be **terrifyingly toothy!** In this book you will meet some of the **biggest** and **best** sharks in the world (from a safe distance, of course!). Which **super shark** will be your favourite?

As you swim through these pages, look out for the SHARK SUSPECTS. Solve the crime by searching for clues in the book. (The criminal will be revealed on page 24!) Ready? Then dive in!

If you do come face to face with a shark, let's hope you're safe inside a shark cage!

Shark Suspects

Sammy the Seal has been attacked! Can you solve the crime?

PAGES 10 TO 11

Shark Spotting

Time to spot some super sharks (if you dare!)

PAGES 12 TO 23

Super Sharks

Sharks are amazing fish which live all over the world. They can be found in every ocean and even in some rivers and lakes. Some sharks swim near the shore and others stay far out at sea. There are over **350** types of shark in the world. Sharks can be as small as a human hand, or as large as a **three-storey building!**

Fin

Most sharks are about the same size as an adult human.

Shark Snacks

Fish Fingers – my favourite!

Many people are scared of sharks because of their teeth! They think they could become a shark snack if they swim in the wrong waters. Not every shark has teeth though, and the ones that do can be fussy about their food.

This is why sharks are famous for their **JAWS** …

- Sharks can have up to **3000** teeth. Each time they lose or break a tooth, another one grows in its place.
- As well as being sharp, some sharks' teeth have a **jagged edge!** Ouch!
- Although they have lots of gnashers, most sharks do not chew their food – they just **tear** it up and **gulp** it down!

The great white shark's teeth are razor-sharp and up to eight centimetres long.

FiSH-FooD FaCT

Sharks do not usually attack people. In fact, humans are more likely to kill sharks than the other way round! When sharks do attack, they think humans are seals or some other fish-food!

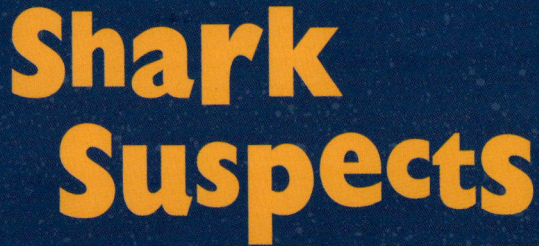

Shark Spotting

NAME: Spined Pygmy Shark

NICKNAME: Shortie

SWIMMING GROUND: The deep waters in temperate (not too hot and not too cold) and tropical (warm) seas around the world.

SHARK SNACKS: Squid, shrimp and other fish.

I'm one of the smallest sharks in the world, but I'm still super! My super shark trick is to **glow in the dark**! I can make my tummy glow and this helps me to hide. Other sharks see the glow, but they don't see me inside it! Clever, huh?

JAWS JOKE

Q: What's the best way to catch a spined pygmy shark?
A: Have someone throw it at you!

NAME: Hammerhead Shark

NICKNAME: Bighead

SWIMMING GROUND: Near the coasts of tropical seas around the world.

SHARK SNACKS: Fish, rays, squid, octopuses and even **other hammerhead sharks!**

JAWS JOKE
Q: Why did the hammerhead shark cross the road?
A: Because it was the chicken's day off.

Just look at my head! Isn't it great? My wide head with eyes at the sides helps me to hunt. I can see nearly all the way round my head, so my victims have nowhere to hide! Once I've spotted my fish-food, I swim towards it really fast and take **huge bites** out of it!

NAME: Bull Shark

NICKNAME: Shovelnose (because its snout is wide and not very long!)

SWIMMING GROUND: Near the coasts of all tropical oceans and seas. They even swim in some freshwater rivers and lakes.

SHARK SNACKS: Fish, rays, turtles, birds and dolphins. Bull Sharks will eat almost anything!

I'm one of the most common types of shark in the seas, so I must be super! But you might not think so! I **attack humans** more than any other kind of shark. This is because I like to swim in shallow water where you like to swim. It's not my fault if you swim into my water! I'm also **very violent**! Sorry, it's just my nature!

JAWS JOKE

Q: Why didn't the bull shark eat the clown?
A: Because he tasted funny!

NAME: Whale Shark

NICKNAME: Bigmouth

SWIMMING GROUND: The tropical oceans and seas around the world.

SHARK SNACKS: Tiny animals in the sea called plankton and krill, as well as small fish and squid.

JAWS JOKE

Q: Why do whale sharks only swim in salt water?
A: Because pepper water makes them sneeze!

I'm the largest shark in the world (I'm not a whale!). But don't be scared of me – I have no teeth! To feed, I swim with my **huge** mouth wide open, sucking in water. Then I close my mouth and use special bristles to sieve the water. This means I can swallow all the animals caught in my bristles and spit out the water. So no big bites from me!

NAME: Great White Shark

NICKNAME: Jaws

SWIMMING GROUND: Near the coasts of most temperate oceans around the world.

SHARK SNACKS: Fish, squid, seals, sea lions, sea turtles, whales and dolphins. The great white shark isn't a fussy eater!

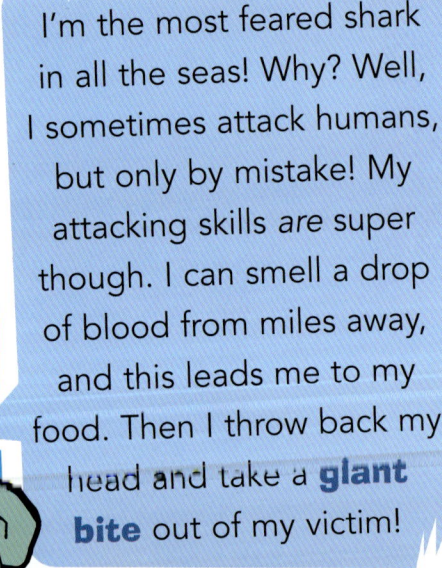

I'm the most feared shark in all the seas! Why? Well, I sometimes attack humans, but only by mistake! My attacking skills *are* super though. I can smell a drop of blood from miles away, and this leads me to my food. Then I throw back my head and take a **giant bite** out of my victim!

JAWS JOKE

Q: What do you get if you cross a great white shark with a cow?

A: I don't know, but I wouldn't want to milk it!

NAME: Megamouth Shark

NICKNAME: Mega

SWIMMING GROUND: Spotted in the Indian, Pacific and Atlantic Oceans.

SHARK SNACKS: Tiny plants and animals found in the sea, like zooplankton, plankton and krill.

JAWS JOKE

Q: Why are megamouth sharks big and grey?
A: Because if they were small and pink, they would be called prawns!

I'm a **very rare** shark. Only **18** of my kind of shark have ever been spotted! But if you see me, you're bound to catch me! I only swim slowly because my **flabby body** and **soft fins** stop me from swimming any faster.

Well, it's safe to go back in the water ... for now. Have you chosen your favourite **super shark**? But more importantly, have you worked out who attacked Sammy the Seal? Well, the criminal of the sea was the only shark in the line-up which likes seals as a shark snack. The **great white shark**! All the other shark suspects are off the hook, but the great white shark is definitely the fishy fiend!